discovermore

Economics in Your Community

Money and Banks

Sloane Wilden

Britannica Educational Publishing
IN ASSOCIATION WITH
THE ROSEN PUBLISHING GROUP

Published in 2024 by The Rosen Publishing Group, Inc.
2544 Clinton Street, Buffalo, NY 14224

Editor: Brianna Propis
Book Design: Michael Flynn

Photo Credits: Cover Michaelpuche/Shutterstock.com; (series background) Dai Yim/Shutterstock.com; p. 4 Seashell World/Shutterstock.com; p. 5 tokar/Shutterstock.com; p. 6 Somchai/Shutterstock.com; p. 7 Smeilov Sergey/Shutterstock.com; p. 8 lego 19861111/Shutterstock.com; p. 9 https://commons.wikimedia.org/wiki/File:Hue-tzu_(Song_Dynasty_government_issue),_1023_-_John_E._Sandrock.jpg; p. 11 (bottom) Sata Productions/Shutterstock.com; p. 11 (top) Cameron Watson/Shutterstock.com; p. 13 Alex Mit/Shutterstock.com; p. 14 PENpics Studio/Shutterstock.com; p. 14 Siarhei Kuranets/Shutterstock.com; p. 15 Che Media/Shutterstock.com; p. 17 (bottom) Africa Studio/Shutterstock.com; p. 17 (top) PKpix/Shutterstock.com; p. 18 Pajor Pawel/Shutterstock.com; p. 19 https://commons.wikimedia.org/wiki/File:Stand_Your_Ground_by_Don_Troiani.jpg; p. 20 (bottom) Jon Kraft/Shutterstock.com; p. 20 (top) Deutschlandreform/Shutterstock.com; p. 23 HANK50/Shutterstock.com; p. 23 Wirestock Creators/Shutterstock.com; p. 24 Real Window Creative/Shutterstock.com; p. 25 Drazen Zigic/Shutterstock.com; p. 26 hanahusain/Shutterstock.com; p. 27 Irina Shatilova/Shutterstock.com; p. 28 panuwat phimpha/Shutterstock.com; p. 29 Parilov/Shutterstock.com.

Library of Congress Cataloging-in-Publication Data

Names: Wilden, Sloane, author.
Title: Money and banks / Sloane Wilden.
Description: Buffalo : Britannica Educational Publishing, [2024] | Series: Discover more: economics in your community | Includes bibliographical references and index.
Identifiers: LCCN 2023030228 | ISBN 9781641900331 (library binding) | ISBN 9781641900324 (paperback) | ISBN 9781641900348 (ebook)
Subjects: LCSH: Banks and banking--Juvenile literature. | Internet banking--Juvenile literature. | Money--Juvenile literature.
Classification: LCC HG1609 .W55 2024 | DDC 332.1--dc23/eng/20230630 -
LC record available at https://lccn.loc.gov/2023030228

Manufactured in the United States of America

CPSIA Compliance Information: Batch #CWBRIT24. For further information contact Rosen Publishing at 1-800-237-9932.

Contents

Connecting Money with Banks

If a person wants to buy a good or service, they often do so with money. In early times, some cultures used shells and beads to "pay," or trade, for things. Money can be almost anything, as long as everyone agrees on its **value**.

One of the earliest forms of money was precious metal, such as gold or silver. Paper money was created as a promise to pay in gold or silver, without having to carry those metals around.

One of the earliest forms of currency were cowrie shells. They were traded for goods and services as early as the 14th century on Africa's western coast.

Banks often have branches where customers can go to ask about or receive services. They can also deposit or withdraw money.

A bank is a business that borrows and lends money. It borrows money from customers called depositors. It lends money to other customers called borrowers.

Banks pay fees to depositors and collect fees from borrowers. The fees are called interest. Banks make a profit by collecting more interest than they pay out. Modern banks offer many other services for their customers.

WORD WISE

VALUE REFERS TO THE AMOUNT OF MONEY AN ITEM IS WORTH. IF THE ITEM IS RARE OR POPULAR, IT WILL MOST LIKELY HAVE A HIGH VALUE.

Currency

Today, coin and paper are the two forms of **currency** most commonly produced. Coins have been around longer than paper money. They were invented before paper money, and they last much longer because they are made of metal.

Banknotes (paper money) are printed on paper that has cotton and other fibers in it. They also are mixed with other materials that make them strong, so they do not tear or fall apart easily. That way, banknotes stay active, or in circulation, longer.

The most common American coins, in order of value, are the quarter, dime, nickel, and penny. They are less than one American dollar and measured in cents.

American paper currency has values of $100, $50, $20, $10, $5, $2, and $1. Any larger bills were discontinued but may still be found.

The blank paper is pressed onto plates filled with ink. This prints the words and pictures that appear on paper currency.

Coins are punched out of sheets of metal. Because there is nothing on the metal at first, the punched coins are called blanks. The blanks are heated, washed, and dried, then the individual designs are printed onto both sides of the blanks.

WORD WISE

CURRENCY REFERS TO THE SYSTEM OF MONEY IN PLACE IN A COUNTRY. AMERICAN CURRENCY HAS COINS AND PAPER BILLS.

When Did We Start Using Money?

Money has been around for the past 5,000 years in some form. In the 600s B.C.E., the kingdom of Lydia, in what is now Turkey, began to make coins. These coins were a combination of silver and gold. The ancient Greeks and the Romans also used coins.

This ancient Lydian coin has an image of a lion printed onto one of its sides.

A banknote is paper money. The first banknotes were developed in China during the 7th century.

The first types of paper money were used in China more than 1,000 years ago. Early paper money was simply a written promise to pay a certain amount of gold or silver money. The paper money was valuable because it could be traded for gold or silver.

Governments later began printing paper money. In the 1900s, most governments made paper money valuable on its own, rather than a bill representing gold or silver.

Consider This

Why do you think America uses both coins and paper money? Why is it important for them to have different values?

The History of Exchange

The original form of exchange—before money—was bartering. This means that people traded things they had for the things they wanted. It was a direct exchange of items for items.

When bartering, each person had to agree that the items being traded had an equal value. For example, a person may have traded five goats for one cow.

People invented money to avoid bartering. Those five goats could be exchanged for a certain amount of money instead of a cow. The money could then be exchanged for grain, cloth, or other goods of the same value.

The value of paper money and coins comes from an agreement between all people regarding their exchange value. Without this agreement, the exchange of money wouldn't work.

In ancient times, animals were often used as a form of currency. Some animals, such as cows and bulls, were worth more than others.

compare and contrast

Using money in exchange for goods or services is more common today than bartering. Is one form of currency more effective than the other?

Two of the most common ways to show that two or more people agreed to an exchange are shaking hands and signing a document.

Metal and Paper

"Use value" is an item that has a practical use, like silver or gold. Silver is used as a backing for mirrors and in making jewelry and electrical products. Gold is used primarily in jewelry. Small amounts of gold are used in other industries, including electronics and dentistry.

When silver and gold are used as money, however, they also have exchange value. They can be exchanged for other things. They are called "hard money" because they are valuable on their own. This is because they are somewhat rare and because they are so useful.

Today most money is in the form of paper or coins made of cheaper metals. The paper and metals are not worth much on their own since they are not rare. There is no limit to the amount of paper that can be manufactured, as long as trees grow. This means paper money and modern coins are not hard money because they are common.

This beautiful necklace is made of gold. Jewelry is one example of precious metals having what is known as "use value."

compare and contrast

How does an item's status of being common or rare affect its use value? Why might a spoon have less value than a silver watch?

Silver is often used in modern dental fillings.

Guarding Money

Not only do certified bills and coins circulate, but counterfeit ones do too. Counterfeit is a term that means a fake copy.

In the past, making counterfeit coins was easy. A cheaper metal of equal weight could be gold- or silver-coated and passed on as real.

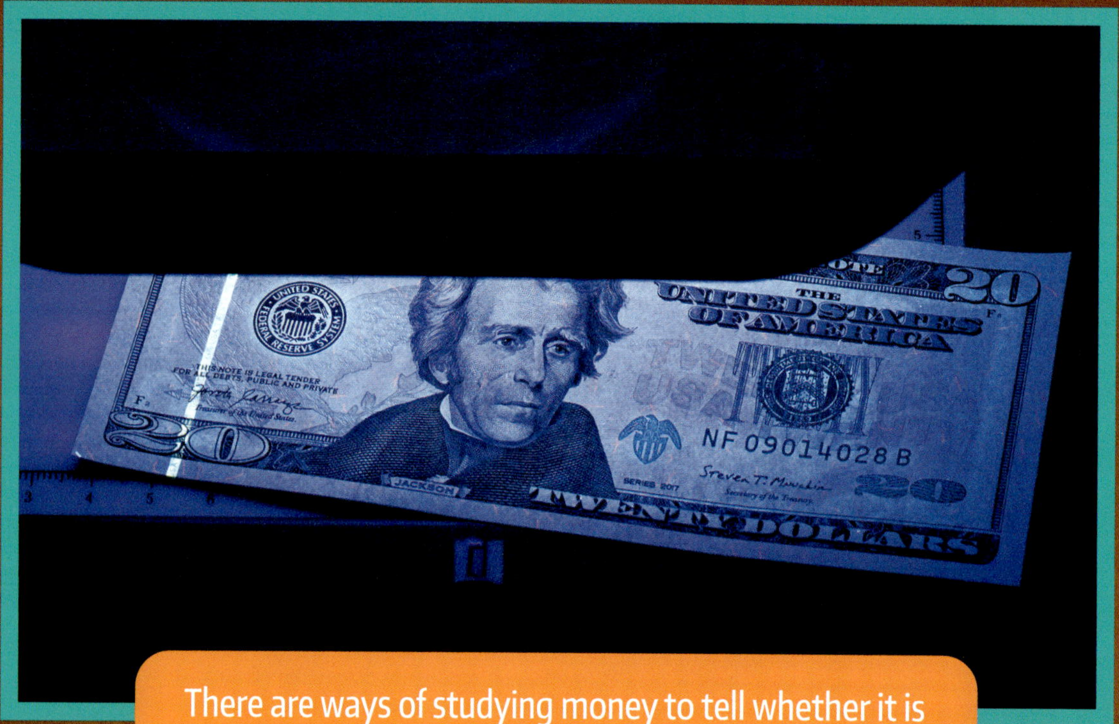

There are ways of studying money to tell whether it is fake or real, such as by holding an ultraviolet light to it.

Holding an American $100 bill up to the light shows the watermark. It is represented by a faint image of Ben Franklin that appears.

Counterfeiting paper money is harder. Nations use special paper and inks to make copying money difficult. The United States uses a very high-quality paper made of cotton and linen. Tiny blue and red silk fibers are woven in to make it even harder to copy.

The paper money of many countries also has a **watermark** on each bill. If a bill does not have these known pieces in place, it is assumed to be fake.

WORD WISE

A WATERMARK IS AN IDENTIFYING DESIGN OR SYMBOL FOUND IN A PIECE OF PAPER ONLY WHEN IT IS HELD UP TO THE LIGHT.

Banking 101

If a person wants to keep their money safe, they can deposit it into a bank. This means putting their money inside the bank. A bank keeps only part of the money in its accounts as cash. It uses the rest to lend to other people and to make investments. Investing means using money to try to make more money.

Banks lend money both to individual people and to businesses. The money borrowed is called a loan. The borrower pays back the loan in portions called installments. The borrower pays the original amount of the loan plus an extra fee called interest.

Modern banks provide other services as well. Many banks issue credit cards and send monthly bills to the people who use them.

Banks also maintain automated teller machines, or ATMs. ATMs can be found in many convenient locations, and they are used to withdraw money from a person's account or to make deposits.

ATMs require a person to enter their pin (personal identification number), often a 4-digit code, to protect their account and the money in it.

compare and contrast

Credit cards can be issued by both banks and businesses. Stores give credit so people will continue shopping at their businesses for goods. Why do you think banks offer customers credit cards?

Bank tellers are employees who are in charge of handling customers' money, such as cashing checks, depositing cash, and collecting payments.

The First Banks

An ancient region in the Middle East called Mesopotamia had a system of banking, at least 4,000 years ago. The first bankers kept gold and silver for people and also lent it out. In ancient Greece and Rome there also were companies very much like modern banks.

Florence and Venice, two cities in Italy, became banking centers in the 1400s. In England, gold dealers served as bankers until the Bank of England was founded in 1694.

When the Bank of England was founded, officials signed a document, called a charter, that detailed what the bank could and could not do.

The Bank of North America was established to aid Congress in providing supplies and money for the troops in the Revolutionary War.

The first bank in the United States was the Bank of North America, which was founded in Philadelphia in 1782. Two years later, it was followed by the Bank of Massachusetts and the Bank of New York.

Some countries have a central bank that oversees all other banks. A central bank also controls the supply of money in the country. In the United States those services are provided by the Federal **Reserve** System, a system established in 1913 that still oversees U.S. banks today.

WORD WISE

BANK RESERVES ARE THE MINIMAL AMOUNTS OF CASH THAT BANKS MUST KEEP IN-HOUSE IN CASE OF AN UNEXPECTED DEMAND.

A Variety of Banks

Commercial banks are the most common type of bank. This type of bank mostly accepts deposits and makes loans. Many commercial banks now offer a number of other products and financial services.

Other kinds of banks do special things. Savings and loan associations make loans to home buyers and owners. International banks lend money to developing countries.

Credit unions are institutions similar to banks. They are formed by people with a common bond such as working for the same company or business. Members of credit unions have a say in the way their union operates. They usually charge lower rates for loans.

Some examples of commercial banks include Bank of America, Citigroup, and Capital One.

compare and contrast

Why might someone choose to use a credit union over a commercial bank or a savings and loan? What are some of the pros and cons of each?

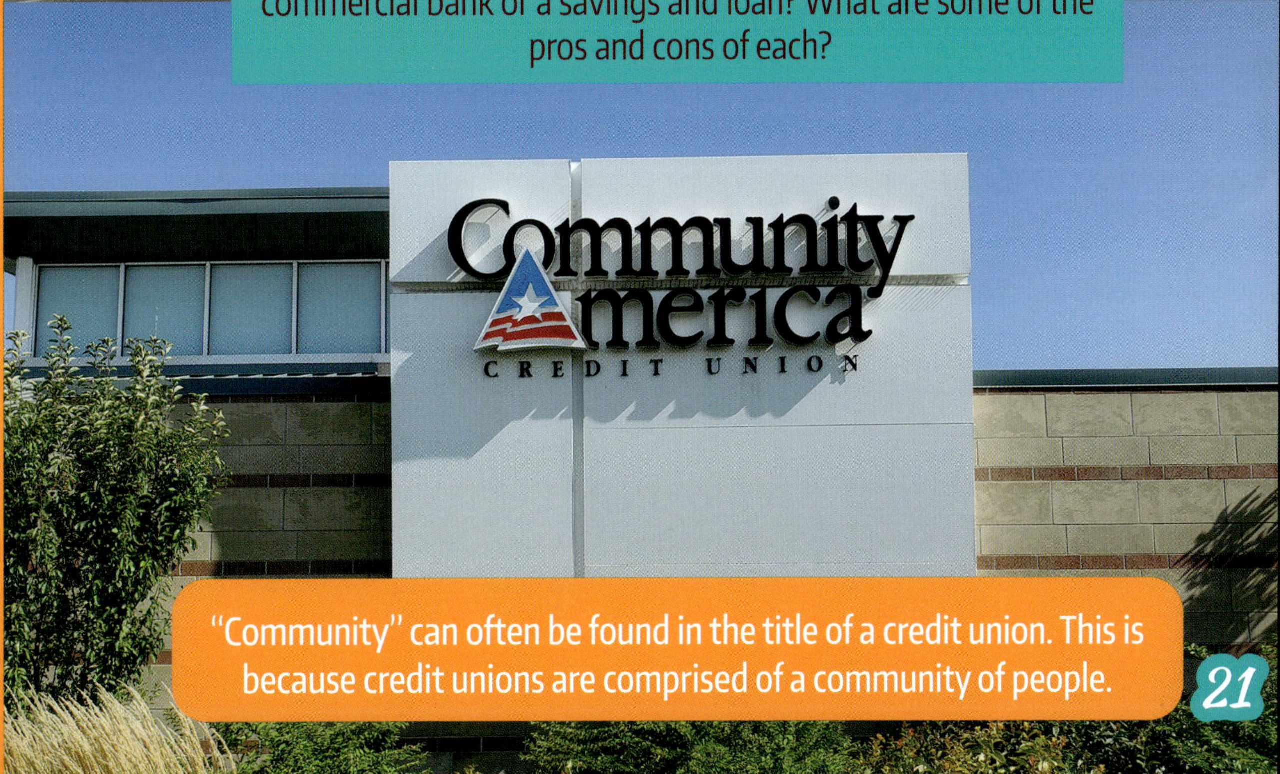

"Community" can often be found in the title of a credit union. This is because credit unions are comprised of a community of people.

The Country's Bank

Central, or reserve, banks are responsible for managing their country's money. They help ensure their country's economic stability and growth.

One of a central bank's most important tasks is deciding how much currency is available to be used. Another key task is setting interest rates. These decisions affect a country's prices and level of employment.

Central banks make sure that the country's private banks are working well. A central bank can lend money to private banks. It may also clear, or process, checks between private banks. In the United States the Federal Reserve System acts like a central bank.

In 1993, a group of countries in Europe formed the European Union. These countries decided to use the same type of currency, called the euro. The European Union created the European Central Bank to oversee the money throughout the union, comprised of 27 member states primarily located in Europe.

The city of Moscow is home to Russia's central bank.

compare and contrast

The central Bank of the United States, founded in 1791, was unpopular. It closed in 1836, and wasn't replaced until 1913 when the Federal Reserve System was established. Why might U.S. citizens not want the government to control the money supply? Why might others be in favor of that?

The euro is the official currency of the European Union. If you travel to Europe and wish to spend money there, you will have to exchange your American currency for euros.

Bank Accounts

When you're able to deposit or withdraw money from a bank, that means you have a bank account. One kind of bank account is a savings account. The bank pays a certain amount of monthly interest for every dollar that someone has in their savings account.

Signing a check is equivalent to signing a written promise to pay for goods and services. Paper money, on the other hand, is a way of paying for the promise.

A man pays his restaurant bill using a debit card. The payment is automatically taken from his checking account.

Another kind of bank account is a checking account. A check is an instruction to the bank to pay out money from that person's account. A person with a checking account can write checks to pay for things. People can also use a debit or check card to pay out money from their checking accounts.

Although checking accounts pay little or no interest to the depositor, they are a protected and helpful way of managing money.

Consider This

Why might a person choose to sign a check to pay for something rather than using paper money?

How Do Banks Operate?

In order to operate and make a profit, banks collect more interest than they hand out. When people deposit money in a bank account, the bank lends some of that money to other people. The bank has to pay interest to the people who make deposits, but the bank makes money when it collects interest on loans.

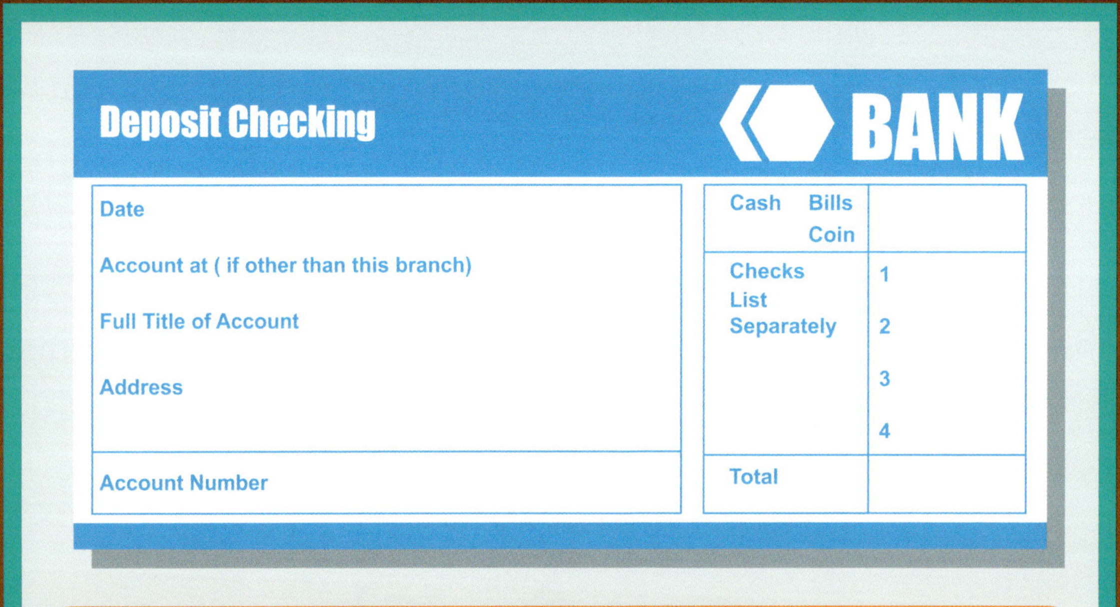

A banking deposit slip is a record of how much money a person puts into their account. It contains the date, the name of the depositor, the depositor's account number, and the amount being deposited.

Another type of bank account that people deposit money into is a savings account. Savings accounts safeguard a person's money and acquire interest.

To have money to loan or invest, a bank must first raise the funds. Deposits are the largest source of a commercial bank's income. Most deposits are made to checking accounts and savings accounts. Banks also offer accounts called certificates of deposit (CDs). These are known as time deposits because they are issued for a certain period of time. People holding CDs agree to let the bank "borrow" their money for that time. At the end of that period, they get their money back plus interest. Interest on CDs is higher than for regular savings accounts.

Banks also raise money through various kinds of borrowing. For instance, a bank may loan money to another bank in need of borrowing it.

Consider This

If a person does not pay their bank loans back on time, what do you think their consequence would be?

Virtual Exchanges

Today banks operate digitally, meaning they use computers and offer the ability to deposit or withdraw money virtually. Customers often use their home computers for banking too. People can pay bills or transfer money between bank accounts over the internet.

Money has gone **digital** too. Bitcoin is a digital currency created in 2009. They exist only on the internet. Owners of Bitcoins can trade them for actual money. They also can exchange Bitcoins for goods and services. They do all of that over a special computer network. The value of Bitcoins depends on how many people want them and how many are available.

Many banks have apps–short for "applications"–that customers can access on their phones for their banking needs.

Bitcoin ATMs can be located in shopping centers, currency exchanges, or other places!

Money and banks may continue to get even more high-tech in the future. But no matter their format, they will remain a crucial way for people to manage their lives and for the economy to thrive.

WORD WISE

DIGITAL, OR VIRTUAL, REFERS TO ANY INTERACTIONS OR PROCESSES CONDUCTED ON THE INTERNET OR WITH ELECTRONICS, SUCH AS A COMPUTER.

Glossary

account Money deposited in a bank.
banknote A piece of paper money.
barter To exchange, or trade, things for other things instead of for money.
blank A coin before it has images and words stamped on it.
borrower One who takes and uses something, including money, with the promise to return it.
circulation The passage of something from person to person or place to place.
counterfeit To imitate or copy for the purpose of tricking someone.
debit card A card used to withdraw money from the holder's bank account immediately at the time of a purchase.
depositor A person who puts their money in a bank.
economic Having to do with making, selling, and using goods and services.
exchange A giving or taking of one thing in return for another.
funds Available money used for a specific purpose.
installments Payments made over a period of time.
interest The price paid for the use of money.
investment Money spent in order to make more money.
issue To send out for sale or circulation.
loan Money lent that is returned with interest.
manufactured Made or created.
profit The gain or benefit from something.
stability A condition in which something is fixed and unchanging.
transfer To pass from one person, place, or situation to another.

For More Information

Books

Baradaran, Mehrsa, Jennifer Goldstein, and Rick Delucco. *A Kids Book About Banking*. Portland, OR: Kids Book About, Inc., 2023.

Flynn, Sarah Wassner. *Not-So-Common Cents: Super Duper Important Facts About Money You Can't Afford to Miss*. Washington, D.C.: National Geographic Kids, 2023.

Kishtainy, Niall. *The Economics Book: Big Ideas Simply Explained*. New York, NY: DK, 2018.

Websites

Banking

www.brainpop.com/math/financialliteracy/banking/

Learn more about banking through informative videos and fun games.

What Is a Bank Account?

www.easypeasyfinance.com/bank-account-for-kids-financial-literacy/

Bank accounts, and their many different forms, are explained here for you to further learn about.

Index